GW00657542

Bird Island

PICTURES FROM A SHOAL OF SAND

LARS JONSSON

Translated by David Christie

CROOM HELM
London & Canberra

© 1983 Lars Jonsson

First published in Great Britain in 1984 by
Croom Helm Limited, Provident House, Burrell Row,
Beckenham, Kent, England

First published in Sweden by Atlantis Publishers

ISBN 0-7099-1443-1

Filmset by Servis Filmsetting Ltd, Manchester

Printed and bound in Denmark

Once upon a time there was a shoal of sand . . .

Resting Little Terns

Summer had already established a hold on the island when my part in this tale begins. Why I waited until then, I do not know for sure: but Spring is in such a hurry; the land is impatient for Summer so that although Spring's vitality and beauty intoxicate me, I seldom manage to do much painting. Everything changes so quickly. My sketchpad is filled with half finished drawings, that partake of the restless unfinished spirit of the season itself. About the time of the Summer solstice when the wild chervil drops its bridal veil, a reflective mood overwhelms me. A mixture of sadness and relief comes over me because Spring and early Summer are ebbing away. Some years the feeling of melancholy is very strong. Already by the middle of June I hear the first Curlews heading south. The meaning of their plaintive cries each year in the same way surprises me and suddenly I am aware of the nearness of death. I feel strongly the echo in the pattern of our own lives. Spring like youth vanishes in an intoxicated moment. When early summer is leaving us, we struggle hard to hold on to it, because at midsummer the poignancy of the approach of autumn is at its most palpable. After midsummer, I achieve a calmer tempo; I accept the passage of time; I pause to rest on my oars, to look around, to reflect – and to paint.

When I speak here of the autumn, the summer is already at its height and its inherent feeling of melancholy has waned. Often I come back to the word 'autumn'. Sometimes it is used as a biological term, an attempt to define conceptually the changing point in nature's yearly course of events. But the word also conveys other, more abstract feelings; feelings about the approaching breaking up of the natural world the power and tension of which it is impossible to explain. The relentless circle of nature is like a human life: we are born with the first spring thaw when the migrant birds return and we die in the late autumn darkness.

But it was of the summer and of the island that I wanted to tell. The Summer solstice had just passed. At a quick glance one day can look very like the next – a summer kaleidoscope of sky and water; the hum of insects and the beat of wings. Most of the birds of the bay have already hatched their young; some are almost full-grown while others are small puffs of down. The island is in fact a sand bar, a long strip of sand stretching into a shallow bay, which is in turn embraced by flat meadows. From a headland on the far side of the bay one can survey the whole landscape. In earlier years I used often to paint from this place. A myriad times my eye has swept over the flat coastal meadows, along the stone dykes and out towards the sea. The feeling of freedom and space is always present. At sea or in open country where the horizon seems to stretch to infinity, our senses are not blocked in any way. It is as though within ourselves the power of the retina to perceive has been transformed and our thoughts and associations can stretch for ever with the horizon out towards the unknown.

Right from the start the island was a natural part of the landscape; it was a part of the system of small islands and headlands which made up the bay itself. The sea, the elevation of the land and the grazing animals change the landscape inexorably but slowly. And so I ask myself how and when was the island formed. Surely a similar formation or an idea of it existed the year before?

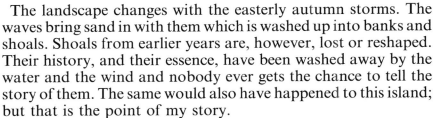

The landscape changes with the easterly autumn storms. The waves bring sand in with them which is washed up into banks and shoals. Shoals from earlier years are, however, lost or reshaped. Their history, and their essence, have been washed away by the water and the wind and nobody ever gets the chance to tell the story of them. The same would also have happened to this island; but that is the point of my story.

I did not suddenly awake to the island's riches. It was by chance that I painted several water-colours using themes from the island. But they formed a pattern; they went together. Instinctively I felt close to a secret passage leading to something surprising. There, as I observed in deep concentration and painted, it began. The paintbrush which worked over the paper and the water-colour which flowed out in patterns and shapes, formed words. I began to see the opening chapters to a thrilling tale.

For a short while birds came to gather strength to continue their migration later. They rested, searched for food and changed their plumage. Young birds grew up, learned to fly and to find food. Plants took root, grew out, flowered and went to seed. The water rose and fell, and formed lines and patterns at the turn of the tide. It brought seaweed and all sorts of flotsam to shore. The winds swept over the sand, reshaped it; brought in new objects and blew away others. Over the island there arched the vastness of the sky where the sun and the clouds always on the move provided ever-changing light patterns. The light came through filters of moistness, warmth, atmospheric pressure and dust and the slightest changes showed in the island's substance, from a mussel shell to the fiery-red bill of a Caspian Tern. The brilliant daylight showed in the fresh, recently washed up bladderwrack; the heaviness in the dark sheets of old seaweed; the silveriness in the terns' pale mantles; the blueness in the shadows of the birds on the sand; the fluctuations between mauve and rose-pink in the algae of the shore zone; everything mirrored the changes of the heavens' canopy.

I came to share the essence of the island. It took on almost religious values for me. Its spectacle fascinated, thrilled, enthralled and entranced me. Each daylight hour that I could not share with it filled me with restlessness. In many respects, what happened on the island was a natural biological progression of events paralleled everywhere in nature. A reality existed, and that reality is the seedbed of emotion and fantasy. Perhaps it was the closeness to nature, the feeling of being allowed to take part in something outside the world of man, that had me spellbound. It does not make much difference, for in this situation the island was an endless sea, an inexhaustible ocean of possibilities. One incident succeeded another, and different chords of colour were sounded, only to float away again. Colours, patterns, movements, expressions, sounds and smells constantly gyrated. I entered into the birds' behaviour, understood their moulting patterns, and understood their unrest just before migration. I took part with more and more intensity in these events so that landscapes from far distant places began to paint themselves right inside me and new events took shape when the wind played in a moulted feather.

I knew exactly how the savanna in west-central Africa must appear to the Ruffs; how it cried out and how they were drawn to it; and how the tundra around the mouth of the Yenisei was now beginning to fall silent. I became one with the birds and with the island's world. A force field arose where impulses constantly flowed between us.

A sketch, a note or a rough list of species can today, (and will always), act as a code through which entire scenes or moods of the landscape can be recaptured afresh. Scientific knowledge in observers and facts shown in pictures can restrict the imagination, but they can also provoke associations outside the plain surface of the pictures. So let your own thoughts run freely away from the base of scientific data and try to pick up new trains. The Knot's slightly transparent brick-red colour, bordering on rosy-pink, and the Curlew Sandpiper's deep brownish-red, as in well-baked brick, vibrate in our minds in different ways. Let your eye wander over the sand and play over its gentle transitions, from the dry sunlit ivory-white to the brownish-mauve, newly wave-washed sand. Different strings of senses are touched; different tones resound and form harmonies.

How can such a small place, a grain of sand on the earth, carry so much within it? The impressions and the motifs are like a fresh summer wind and the water-colour paper like a sailcloth. I try to catch the wind and hoist my sails. They are filled, and as they billow to the brim we are carried out to the open sea, while the wind itself merely surges further afield, unfettered in its abounding possibilities.

The pictures and the text follow the events of the summer. They are the images of inspiration. No thought or perception inspired by the pictures is untrue. Nothing can be proved because the island is gone for ever. All that is left is my account, these impressions from the island's short summer lifetime.

To the memory of my friend the painter Allan Andersson, whose painter's heart was inspired by the life of meadows by the sea

First landing

Bird islands are special places. There is a feeling of space but with unusual features. This is especially true of sand shoals, islets or rock skerries where human beings never go and the birds breed everywhere. There the ground is imprinted with the goings-on of the birds – it is their world.

Today for the first time, I visited the island wading out in the warm water. The ground beneath me was soft, rather oozy and I could feel beneath my feet the small, delicate, twisted knots of some plant. I landed on the southwest tip. As soon as I put my bare foot down on the warm sand a sudden feeling passed through me that I was trespassing. It was like entering somebody else's house in the owner's absence. Even if one has permission and good reason to enter, there is still a strange feeling of having no right to be there, as if one were claiming to be another person. It is almost with a feeling of shame that one quickly carries out one's mission and sneaks away. At first, however, I stood fascinated and allowed my eyes to look about over the sand, along the shoreline and over the small communities consisting of sea sandwart and sea arrowgrass. My footsteps felt like an elephant's in a doll's house. The pebbles and the sand were flattened down and disturbed by the tramping of thousands of birds' feet. Feathers, down and excrement bound the whole area together. I tried to be light of foot and to walk on the seaweed and veins of gravel where the tracks appeared fewer. It turned out to be a short visit. I took a little seaweed, dried seagrass and some shells as my artist's props and began my journey back. I could not, however, help stopping for one more time and simply letting my senses feel everything. My eyes looked over the sand, registered the vibrant play of colours created by the thousands of

grains of sand, pebbles and shells. Suddenly, from out of the surface area, the form of four eggs barely the size of a walnut appeared in a shallow scrape: a Ringed Plover's nest.

The whole visit took perhaps two minutes.

Ringed Plover's nest

Sand

Life has its different faces on the island. The stage is sand, soft fine-grained sand which is washed up in the backwater of the currents, coarser sand which, like the flat ridges of pebbles, lies where it has been deposited on the outer side, wavy strings of finer gravel and isolated pebbles. The sand lies there, washed up like silt under the ever-watchful sky, and accepts whatever chooses to land, drop down or be washed up.

Stretched out, like a wooden club or monkey-wrench in shape, perhaps like a stratified thigh-bone from some prehistoric giant animal, it just lies there. Eighty-one paces long and thirty-one paces at its broadest.

Along its length runs a barely visible ridge where the coarser sand and the pebbles have collected. Deposited here are old sheets of seaweed, strings of sea-mussel shells and a couple of boards, a few pieces of wood and other bits and pieces, including an old bundle of plastic. The terns nest here and often rest in the shelter of the ridge. The strips of seaweed with their broken pattern make a good camouflage for several of the young birds.

The north end is shaped like a cross-section of a young boletus fungus with small pools of water in the undersides of 'the cap'. A mixed flock of gulls and terns rests here daily. Out towards the northeast runs an underwater reef of sand which comes to light at low water. The southwest tip also extends into an underwater reef which stretches in a long curve. Oystercatchers and Bar-tailed Godwits often search for food here.

Along the outer side, facing the sea, miniature spits of seaweed and seagrass are formed which are periodically very productive feeding places for most of the waders. The water off here is very shallow and the bottom pure sand. On the west side and in the inner bay the water is often more cloudy, richer in food, and the bottom more muddy. Here a kind of small bay, a cove, has been created which is the most important feeding area for the majority of the waders and the few ducks that come. The beach at the cove rises fairly steeply in a half-metre-wide slope.

The southwest tip is nearest to firm land, and here there are several clumps of various grasses and plants. The clumps in the water are more solid in character and must have originated at least a couple of years back. They are popular resting places for certain waders, among others Dunlin, Redshank and Avocets.

The island is populated by birds, some residents; others are on passage and rest for shorter or longer periods. It made me think of an international airport. Not only because it provides an intermediate resting place for those on passage to and from exotic places all around the world, but also because its extension and shape in the flat open landscape remind me of a runway.

The calls are like different languages. Well-known or strange tongues from different peoples and populations are mingled. They travel alone, in groups or in large parties. A group of Russians chat while searching for food, while a lone traveller sleeps standing up or carries out his morning toilet. Some eager to get away, while others rest calmly, awaiting their departure. Some will not travel at all, and carry out their daily routine quite unaffected by the travellers streaming through.

The whole scene is dominated by gulls and terns. The Little Terns are the most numerous and now, at the end of June, have half-grown young. Two pairs of Arctic Terns, at least one of which has nested here, and several Common Terns are among the daily visitors.

The Black-headed Gulls doze on the northern tip for several hours in the middle of the day. Life is easy for a gull when breeding is finished with and the summer is rich in food.

Ringed Plovers had failed with an earlier brood; perhaps some gull was to blame, or their nest was washed out by a high tide. Now they have a new clutch. The female sits for a greater part of the time; her colours are a shade duller than her mate's.

The male defends the territory; the message in his colour pattern cannot be misunderstood.

Ringed Plover: the male stands in defence of his territory

Common Tern

Resting Black-headed Gulls

6 July

Calm evening, the first Dunlins and six Bar-tailed Godwits fly south. Cloud over the bay after a warm day.

Ringed Plover

8 July

When I arrive in the morning the Ringed Plovers have hatched; one of the chicks is already dry and is rooting about under the female's belly feathers. The others probably hatch during the day, for in the afternoon I see at least three of them making short trips around the nest. But they soon come back and are swallowed up in the female's underfeathers.

The young hatch at intervals of several hours. The eggs are laid at intervals of about one day, but incubation does not begin until the fourth egg so that hatching takes place more or less at the same time. The eggs are brooded for a good four weeks, so the female must have laid some time around 10 June. Normally Ringed Plovers lay in April and May, but repeated failures can cause them to lay as late as August.

The Ringed Plovers have hatched

Arctic Tern

9 July

Sun, warm easterly winds, and the harsh, slightly nasal chatterings of the Little Terns roll over the island. There were twenty-one standing on or flying around the island.

Arctic and Common Terns are so similar, yet so different. They are difficult to tell apart in the field, but when one has got to know them, they cannot be confused. The Arctic Tern is elegant, silver-grey with a blood-red bill and short, almost negligible legs. The Common Tern is grey, with a significantly stronger carrot-red bill which can take slightly larger fish. The legs can always be seen when it is standing. In the air both species are as elegant as ice-dancing couples, where the Arctic Tern is the female partner who denies the laws of gravity with her lightness, rhythmics and natural grace, while the Common Tern flies with more vigour and energy. The differences in the young are just as marked. The young Arctic has a doll-like prettiness with its dark bill and dark-set eyes. The Common Tern has something of a young gull about it, slightly deformed and with brilliant light orange bill.

The Arctic Tern's young is out swimming in shallow water and picking small insects on the surface – the beginnings of fishing on its own? Yesterday it was rooting about near a piece of plastic flotsam, plucking plucking small creeping insects from it. This interest in everything small that moves is still a game, but in a few weeks will become an essential skill when it will be finding its own food.

An adult Arctic Tern is also bathing, walking out into the water deep as its belly, snapping in the water and then beginning its toilet. As a human being, who first washes his hands, arms and face before bathing, a bird begins its bath by dipping its bill. The tern continues by crouching and dipping its belly, bows tentatively a few times, lowers its head and lets the water run over its back. At the peak it swings deep into the water, spreads its feathers and hangs its wings so that the water can get in between the feathers. Now and again it balances on its side and splashes hard with its wing so that there is a great shower of spray. When it is finished it flies up and shakes itself off in the air, ruffles its whole body, at the same time drops ominously but beats its wings again just above the surface of the water.

The Avocet has four young, only a couple of days old. She searches for food with her young in the cove or the channel between the island and the shore. The pair is ever watchful, and they frantically chase off Common Gulls that fly past. Now and then the female warms the young in her belly feathers. To reach the right level she has to get down on her knees. All four disappear into the downy feather bed so that nothing other than four pairs of legs is visible, a comical sight and bewildering if one does not immediately realise what is going on.

The Avocet warms its young

10 July

I had to drive in to town and did not come down to the island until about five o'clock in the afternoon.

A light east wind, calm, a slight atmosphere of suspense as there should be at the end of a warm day. Delightful, the shadows are distinct but still a little hazy at the edge from the lingering warmth. An adult White Wagtail is catching insects among the grass and one of the fledged young is squatting down and confidently awaiting its evening meal.

The evening comes quickly. Perhaps a subjective observation since I had not been able to get down here for the whole day. The coast is set in a rosy-red bed, between water and sky. Dusks at the end of warm, gentle summer days are rose-pink in the North; cold, fresh dusks are yellow. Under cover of darkness new shapes now arrive, and the summer-night scene unfolds. A hard raucous call pierces the air and a Grey Heron lands on lanky legs immediately off the northeastern tip of the island. Terns and waders take flight, alarmed by the large expanses of wing, and when they land shortly afterwards the heron takes off again

– unsettled by my presence? Not exactly too neat an entrance, but peace is soon restored and suddenly I see that several herons have taken its place. The sea has an amazing capacity for reflecting the faint light of the dusk and dawn skies. Against the water I can make out the slender bodies and reptile-like patterns of movement of the herons. After having spent the whole day standing like wreckage on an islet farther away, they have now begun their hunt for food. Their behaviour reveals that something is happening under the surface of the water. Under cover of darkness the shallow, lukewarm summer bays are invaded by thousands of fishes.

Far off there is a light shining in a window. Some secluded cottage where summer guests are playing some game? – there's no way I can know. Maybe somebody is sitting on the doorstep enjoying the fragrance of jasmine, and pulling a shawl around the shoulders when the first cool air of twilight makes itself felt. It looks cosy in any case, but we in the bay are in another world where a thousand fish eyes, a dozen herons and I are trying to make the most of the night.

11 July

They are now three days old, weigh perhaps fifteen grams, and run as fast as I walk. They make frequent excursions between the band of seaweed where they rest, four–five metres up on the island, and the water's edge. Their movements are those of their parents in miniature: they balance on their footsteps, snatch insects, scratch themselves and stretch their small wings. When they scratch themselves with one leg, they often lose their balance and have to spread their wings and abandon the whole exercise in order not to tumble over. It has a very precocious look about it, and of course that's what it is, too. Like the young of most waders, they are able to search for food completely on their own.

Ringed Plover chicks

The Oystercatcher's young, unlike the Ringed Plover's, is fed at regular intervals. But it also picks up a few small animals for itself at the water's edge or up on the island. For a large part of the day it lies low, huddled against a clump of seaweed or seagrass matching its rather dark brownish-grey colour. When one of its parents probes for worms along the outer side of the island, the young immediately comes running and follows hard on its heels.

The Little Tern's young has satisfied its hunger and takes a walk over the sand. One parent has arrived with food and follows after it, enticing it with a little silvery fish in its bill. But the young merely settles up against a clump of seaweed and demonstrates quite clearly its lack of interest. The adult bird goes over to it and continues to insist 'a spoonful for mummy . . .'. Suddenly it is chased off by another Little Tern, quickly and effectively. To whom does the young belong? Maybe the first tern had made a mistake and tried to feed one of a neighbouring pair's young, or maybe it had lost its own chick.

The young sinks deeper down into the sand, and merges with the hazy white midday light.

Oystercatcher

Little Tern young

All of a sudden three Curlew Sandpipers stand in the cove, the first of the year and in full summer plumage. Their brilliant colour has an exotic feel and I am captivated by them the whole afternoon. While I draw and paint, I see how the water level changes. Sheets and strips of seaweed are now uncovered, now vanish. The sky and the sand are reflected in the water, diffracted in the shimmering zones around the wet seaweed. Just before sunset they fly on on south.

Six Bar-tailed Godwits rest for a short time during the afternoon. All but one have just started to moult. The impression they convey is of a slightly blended beige-grey and rust-red. Restless, they walk towards the northeast tip, take off and fly towards the inner bay. My telescope follows them to the beach. For several days I have been seeing gliding Bar-tailed Godwits from behind; the wings are always angled downwards.

12 July

I hear a Whimbrel calling over the sea. I look for it for some time before I find twelve large waders against the slightly dull afternoon sky. These are Curlews, eleven individuals, and a single Whimbrel which is hanging on in tow, noticeably smaller and with quicker wing beats. It is not unusual in wader flocks to hear one odd member of another species calling intensely. The Whimbrel is looking for its own species and calls its message down over the bay, while the Curlews silently work their way southwestwards. In the same way, for example, ten Sanderlings in a flock of a hundred Dunlins can make the most noise; they must have sound contact so as not to lose one another.

When the flocks of large waders pass here, they slow down their speed and call – the march is on! They are after a minimum possible speed without losing too much height, and long, slightly descending gliding stages are backed up by series of short rapid wing beats. The flock, strung out in a line, surges when the series of wing beats passes from the front backwards through to the rear. Now and then one bird pumps almost imperceptibly with its outer wing, the hand, in the gliding stage in order to maintain height and direction, so that the aerodynamics are not broken, so that the rhythm is sustained.

When at about seven o'clock I get up and leave the lee of the stone dyke, I can feel that the wind has begun to freshen. Summer weather, certainly, but not the obvious and tender early part of summer. For the first time the humidity and spray from the sea tell that summer does not last for ever, that it also has another side. Most would say high summer, but I think of it as migration weather. There is a funny feeling in my body that the year is inexorably turning and that the great migration south is beginning.

I hardly manage to think this thought when I see twenty or so small waders in the inner bay. A quick sweep, yes indeed! The year's first Little Stint. In full summer dress, warm rusty-orange and ochre. The rest are Dunlins and four Curlew Sandpipers. These arctic waders, wanderers from far-distant lands, come every day now to visit the bay; some rest in small flocks close to the island, others merely pass through.

Little Stint

A Knot is resting on the island, completely grey and probably a year-old non-breeding bird. These one-year-old birds seldom accompany the others up to the arctic breeding grounds and consequently do not assume a summer plumage but instead another winter plumage, perhaps with a few traces of summer colours.

In the inner bay stood six Bar-tailed Godwits, one of which, a female, has now been here for three days. They slept, cleaned themselves and sought food. At about five o'clock in the afternoon they moved on, beckoned up by some Curlews which called as they passed. The island's 'regular female', however, was left behind. Had she chosen to moult here, or was she sick or in poor condition?

Thirty seconds later I heard several rapid nasal 'nott nott' calls – Knot. A bird passing by has discovered the other member of its species on the island and is winging down from the sky. It flies hesitantly, at a reduced speed in a tight circle around the island, like a model aircraft held back by a wire from the centre but driven outwards by the centrifugal force. The outcome is not long in coming: the resting Knot takes off, and with rapid shearing wing beats, up it goes alongside and joins in the orbit of the circle. On the far side its ties to the island are released and, as in a straight after the final bend, the two birds pick up speed, tremendous speed. Close to the water, all the while accelerating, and at perhaps fifty miles an hour, they disappear out towards the southeast. The whole manoeuvre takes maybe ten seconds, ten seconds of the journey between the tundra of the Arctic Ocean and some west European or African estuary.

A minute later I hear Bar-tailed Godwits again; I look up and see three godwits and a Knot gliding in across the sky from the south. They drop, fly in a wide semicircle around the bay, look like alighting on the island, hesitate, make an attempt to land on the point, but continue out over the sea where I lose them from view. In all probability they came in from the northeast and were attracted first by the bay and later by the lone female Bar-tailed Godwit on the island. She did not have sufficient power of attraction to suppress their migratory fervour.

Ten minutes later a flock of Dunlins arrives. They divide up: twelve fly farther south, and five alight on the island for a few seconds but change their minds and quickly move off after the main group. A score of Dunlins that have stayed all day, however, quietly remain there.

Adjustments are constantly taking place between different wills and different states of readiness for migration. When some in the flock are prepared to rest, other – perhaps more experienced – members have made up their minds to carry on farther, maybe to a place they already know from earlier years. Does the will of the younger members stand in the way of the experience of the collective assembly?

Studies of Dunlins

Dunlins

Isolated grating croaks from Dunlins seem to fill the whole air. I look up towards the clouds, and high up there a tight flock travels on a course as straight as an arrow to the southwest. For a long time I listen and look up at this sky filled with long-billed, plump and earnest Siberian Dunlins.

A flock approaches and passes over the island. From out of the group ringing 'krilli' calls are heard; two Curlew Sandpipers come into the field of view through my binoculars just as they land on the sloping shore near the cove. They stand rigid for a few short seconds, take a few quick nervous steps towards the ridge but take off at once. The air is vibrant with migration unrest.

Eyes **B**lack little eyes, eager to observe, are turned towards the sky. This clear unending canopy is mirrored in and interpreted by thousands of small dark eyes. Our vast space is their roadway. What for us is air, endlessness and intangible is for them a plan of action, a chart covered with symbols. Up there, calls are heard and thousands of wings beat. Each movement and flight activity, each silhouette and call, forms a web of stimuli, a kind of diagram. When suddenly all coefficients coincide for the individual or the flock, they take flight. I can distinctly feel the suction, the draught, when twelve Grey Plovers in hurried flight describe a perfectly straight line southwestwards across the afternoon sky.

Knot

39

21 July

Dull, with grey clouds moving fast across the sky, northeast wind, several degrees colder than normal and with rain in the air – Tringa-weather. Yes, one has the instinctive feeling that certain waders of the genus *Tringa* are off on migration. And sure enough, the scene is dominated by young Wood Sandpipers in the company of solitary Greenshanks and Common Sandpipers. I have just settled down when fifteen Wood Sandpipers move over the island in loose formation. Wood Sandpipers seldom form tight flocks; they have a strong sense of individuality. They often fly in small groups, and a relatively large flock of fifteen birds forms an elongated oval or ellipse. The more purposefully they are migrating, that is to say the more common their goal, the more tightly they pack themselves together. In this way one can read how motivated the flock is, how strong their common migratory urge is.

Ringed Plover chick

When searching for food, they establish small territories, small individual spaces, within which the presence of others is not tolerated. Their food consists of insects and small animals which are picked from the surface of the shore zone and which they locate by sight. It is just the same with us; when we go picking mushrooms or berries, we quite naturally spread out, for if our fields of view overlap arguments can break out. The Dunlins on the other hand pack tightly together, for they do not see their food, they feel it with their bills, probe for it in seaweed and mud.

I am sitting painting a Dunlin that is standing asleep in the seaweed when it begins to rain. In the still water at the edge of the shore where the seaweed has built breakwaters, I can see the rain fall. It starts as a dry drizzling, a fine haze of dust-like rain. Then a steady rain that makes visible rings on the water. The rain continues to come down steadily but fluctuating in intensity, and everything becomes wet. After an hour it eases, but just before it does large, heavy drops fall which form small cascades on impact, like the last heavy drops when one turns off a water tap. The rain has its phases, its rhythm, its dynamics.

Young Wood Sandpiper

Snipe, late afternoon

Young White Wagtail

23 July

It is about five o'clock in the afternoon, the sun is shining and the day's fresh south wind had dropped. A warm and peaceful atmosphere pervades the island, a summer atmosphere. The birds appear not to be in such a hurry to migrate; they look perfectly comfortable in the warm sand and seaweed. I count exactly one hundred birds. When on one occasion they are put up, I see that a further thirty birds have been standing concealed behind the ridge.

At least ten White Wagtails are chasing insects over the sand. They nod as they walk, slightly crouched, tails bobbing up and down. Since flying insects are easier to detect when silhouetted against the sky, they crouch down and put their heads on one side, then make either a bouncing leap or a swift rush.

In all, a rather amusing ballet over a gigantic stage.

A flock of Turnstones alights on the island, mostly young birds and possibly from the neighbourhood. They appear somewhat agitated and on several occasions they fly around in a tight flock and call, obviously with travel jitters. Throughout the evening they move around anxiously uttering short, rapid 'kvitt' and 'tjutt' calls – short, sort of podgy calls, like the birds themselves. Just before dark they take wing for the last time, disturbed by something I cannot detect. Seconds later, however, I hear a jet-plane. A steel bird perhaps influences their fate, causes them to fly farther and not to spend the night on the island. Maybe their different routes eventually cross somewhere down around the Mediterranean Sea or in Africa?

Studies of Turnstones

24 July

It becomes cloudy and rainy towards evening, exactly as the weather forecast has promised; cold-front on the way. I drive down in the late dusk and light rain, and walk several kilometres over the shore meadows. 'Cold-front' – it never feels so warm as when the weather gets cloudy after a hot and close day. Humid warmth tenderly wrapping itself around me – it makes me think of the tropics. The rain releases all the smells from the shore heath. They lie heavy in the air as in a farmhouse kitchen.

I steal up behind a stone dyke in the hope of seeing geese on the island. The Redshanks, however, give away my intrusion, and sound the warning with their persistent, beating calls. Soon I have several birds alarm-calling above my head, even though I had taken the usual route.

The darkness turns fact into fiction. Nature's spirit frees itself. The water level is low, the island has risen, and it feels as if I have caught it by surprise in the darkness of night. It almost touches the shore, and if one did not sink down in the soft bottom sand one would be able to reach it with dry feet. The island's beings – molluscs, clumps of seaweed and small bits of wreckage – can creep up to land and carry out their missions. Here, a secret exchange takes place.

A brood of Shelducks hastens across the island and enters the water on the other side. Three Shovelers in the cove stretch their necks a little but choose to stay. I can make out five Curlew Sandpipers on the beach. How marvellous their colour is! It is so dark that I can barely distinguish any colours at all, but the Curlew Sandpipers' deep rust-red colour penetrates the gloom. The colour is in no way the red of a Robin Redbreast, but it is Robin Redbreast that I find myself thinking of. Last week the Curlew Sandpipers were wandering about on vast desolate expanses of tundra where meltwater ran steadily down towards the Arctic Ocean, as near to the North Pole as one can get on dry land; perhaps they have come from places where no human being has ever set foot. Now they are standing here in the dissolute dark grey summer night, the tundra's Robin Redbreasts.

On my way home, I see a little white sprite moving around at grass-top height. Scared out of its wits by the tramping of human footsteps, it dashes nervously and with lightning-fast turns above the grasslands. If there had not been thunder in the air I would have thought that it was a white tiger-moth or some evening fluke, but now it is a sprite.

Curlew Sandpipers

Drawing geese

Each day I see the goose droppings on the island increase more and more. Snake-like piles of decaying matter lie there. Only once when I crept up behind the wall, have I caught a glimpse of them.

Today I go down to the shore meadows and approach the island from the northwest. Yesterday evening's rain had not come to much, it had not turned into any real downpour. The air is still heavy and humid. It is cloudy but all the time the sun is trying to break through, giving bursts of light and warmth. The time is around seven, there is still a little of the morning in the air and the haze envelops the bay in a milky back-light. About forty Greylag Geese take off from the inner waters, pass directly above me and land in the bay. I settle myself on a boulder

and slowly sweep my telescope over the bay, where the low water reveals hundreds of pebbles and several small tussocks and islets. About one hundred and fifty geese are standing in the water, spread out in small groups. Five of them are standing on the island, in a ponderous and dignified manner, nicely arranged on the northwest tip. They are preening and sleeping randomly.

In a place such as this in the middle of July, Greylag Geese have already moulted. They prepare themselves before the journey southwards. As early as August they have disappeared from this region. The main cause is wild-fowling, for after the first 'open' weekend at the end of July all are gone.

It is difficult to draw and paint geese. They have volume and heaviness like few other birds, which makes them exciting subjects for rough sketches. They are the clumsy cows of the bird world, with full breasts, slightly haycockish bellies and sculptural heads. Their gait is leisurely and circumspect, and they are heavy on their feet. In the haze I see them as grey silhouettes or shimmering bronzes. Their dignity becomes even more prominent with the distance and the light. The essence of their character becomes clearer the longer I watch them, the more the back lighting increases and the rising sun causes their outlines to shimmer.

Sandwich Tern

28 July

They are just standing there as naturally as all the other birds, but they come as a surprise to me. I know of their presence in the area, have often seen and heard them – but never as guests on the island. A white mist flows in towards the beach, telling that sea and air are not in harmony. Is it possibly this tension that has changed the Caspian Terns' daily routine? Their bulk appears to be greater in the mist, and they have the innate natural dignity of Roman marble busts.

Caspian Terns

29 July

It is raining, heavily. Sky and sea are grey. The Redshank's young also looks grey, the same bird which under other circumstances has had such a pretty warm brownish-beige tone. In the light of grey weather, it is stones and sand that stand out. Their pink, ochre and brown tones blossom and increase in value.

Several Grey Plovers have dropped down out of the sky with the rain. Many waders migrate at high altitude and pass by here completely unnoticed, but the bad weather has forced them down today. Each Grey Plover hunts by itself.

Its feeding territory has a radius of five to ten metres and intruding members of the same species are immediately chased away. Only when resting do they stand more closely together.

Suddenly all birds take off, as if on a command. Instinctively I look up from the boulder and search for what has caused the alarm. After a few seconds I see a dark shadow come into view out of the rain haze out over the sea – Arctic Skua. Like a falcon, or even more lithe, it flies in over the point, makes a few rapid wing beats and glides towards the island. Terns and waders pitch to and fro in tight formations. The Arctic Skua singles out a Sandwich Tern, makes several rapid attacks, but soon breaks off 'the game'. It did not turn into any serious attempt. It turns in a wide sweep and resumes its journey out over the sea. Skuas parasitise gulls and terns by attacking them so that they release their catch or regurgitate their stomach contents. Few birds are so well proportioned and have such good coordination as skuas. Long after calm has settled on the island the scene lingers before my eyes.

Arctic Skua

30 July

I paint the grass and the plants against the eventide light. Then I again notice that leaves and blades of grass in the meadows are grazed and blunted, something which struck me the day before yesterday. The sea asters, whose pale lilac flowers I have waited for, were also cropped. I had not given any reasonable second thoughts to the phenomenon; I had taken it quite for granted that it was the geese.

Just before sunset three of the young beasts wade out on to the island and the mystery is solved, quite obviously. They squelch around in the sand and graze a little around the tufts. When I get them in my telescope out on the island, what I see surprises me. I had focused on a level with the birds. Their 'little' world, their faces, expressions and goings-on were the reality. When now these colossi of flesh and blood wallow in on the scene, everything is stood on its head, like the scene of an invasion from an alien planet. They were quite beyond my expectations. The experience of the large bodies, the volumes, silhouetted against the faint yellow evening sky is powerful and beautiful.

The image of the island which I had nurtured in myself, I could still subconsciously recapture; but the cows did not enter into it. Their visit to the island was of course completely natural, something one should have anticipated, but their visit opens up a new world. Not only the cows in themselves, but the feeling that a new dimension has been discovered. The excitement that intellectually I knew existed was exchanged for real excitement. Painting a picture of the island is not the same as painting a picture from the island, from the great field of tension that arises between the subject and my awareness of it, my thoughts, impressions and senses.

An odd cloud hangs high in the sky, creamy-yellow from the rays of the setting sun.

Young White Wagtail on the hunt for insects

56

It is late, around ten o'clock in the evening. The sky still has a mid-blue colour which in the west fades first to turquoise then to yellowish and pink. Towards the blackish-blue horizon there is a dull lilac band. The sky often appears light in the dusk, in contrast with the dark landmass. In the west, down beside the bay, it is blackish-blue and almost completely without any markings; only the ripe tufts of grass are luminous, billowing in the wind. I reflect on all this while I linger in my car – captivated by a tune on the radio. The experiences intermingle strangely; I note down the lines: 'When it's darkness in the delta, when the heaven is on my side, when it's darkness in the delta let me linger in the night.'

The island lies stretched out in the water like a gigantic prehistoric lizard; its dorsal ridge is jagged from the silhouettes of throngs of birds. They take wing when I appear, and from the confusion of wings one group of birds detaches itself; these at once stand out by their particular flight. They dance in tight formation and proceed in the direction of the island, while the other birds land in an erratic fluttering of wings. 'Dance' is the word. In flight the ten birds, barely as large as Arctic Terns, alternately float gracefully several metres above the water and then stretch out in a line close above the surface in swift rhythmic flight. They move in a wide semicircle around the northwest corner and then speed off towards the southeast, towards the sea. These relatively small birds dissolve almost at once against the sea, roughly outlined by blackish-blue wave crests.

They do not belong to the usual set of birds on the island. This can be seen, and is emphasised, by the fact that they are in such a hurry to get out of sight. For a long time I stand and wonder what they can have been, from which remote fenland or Arctic Ocean delta do they come? Again I am gripped by the feeling of having witnessed something which was not intended for human eyes – then all of a sudden they return, effortlessly dancing in over the island. Is the night out there too dark, too off-putting? In the very second they are swallowed up by the black body of the island I hear a couple of short 'kerre' calls . . . of course, Black Terns.

A heron comes in with deep cupped wings and lands on the outer side, standing like an elegantly chiselled African wood sculpture, stylised, caricatured.

In the evening the Teals come, the night is their time

Studies of preening Avocets

1 August

The air is warm, thundery. The island is stationed between sultry airmasses over Russia and cold in the west. A white haze brings soft colours to the landscape. High water, and sea foam is formed against the shore, white bodies which gently slither up the sand like large molluscs. The rhythmic ebb and flow of the waves makes them breathe, heavily and rapidly – just as we pant when brought to the edge of exhaustion. It is night and a giant turtle, a prehistoric leftover, is perhaps at this very moment heaving its body onto some far-distant sandbank. 'My' turtle, well up the beach, sinks flat against the sand and dies like a jellyfish on the shore. The wind tears into it and blows away some fragments, which roll in over the sand; the fertilisation is done.

Sea foam and seaweed are brothers. The sea is warm and the gentle waves of late summer bring seaweed with them. Mountains are formed along the outside of the island, and bunches lie tossed out over the sand; soggy brownish-black sheets form patterns. The waves have washed them far in over the dry sand. Had the Ringed Plover still been sitting on eggs, the nest would have been washed over by the waves at some time during the night. Life is suspended on a fragile thread.

Breathing space

Warm overcast, muggy, calm. A heavy atmosphere. Not a breath of wind, still, greyness, suspense. We are facing a turning point; and the final breakthrough of autumn. The air feels heavy; the bay is full of birds, their movement only adding to the stillness. A few curlews squeeze themselves through the air. Isolated birds call, but the air quickly closes up again. Greenshank, Grey Plover, a distant Great Black-backed Gull, Lapwing, Swallow, all call their message. Time stands still; for a few minutes, a vacuum is created by the changing weather. One is almost afraid to breathe, knowing full well that at any moment the wind will get up; rain fall, clouds open up, releasing the elements from their bondage. A crucible where everything is enclosed, human beings, animals, plants, rocks, all creation. A plaintive and vibrating call from a young Curlew bursts the bubble, and an east wind cools the cheek and gently begins to stir the blades of grass. I shake my head a little and wonder if really it was the Curlew that set the wind free or if it was the wind that set free a pent-up call.

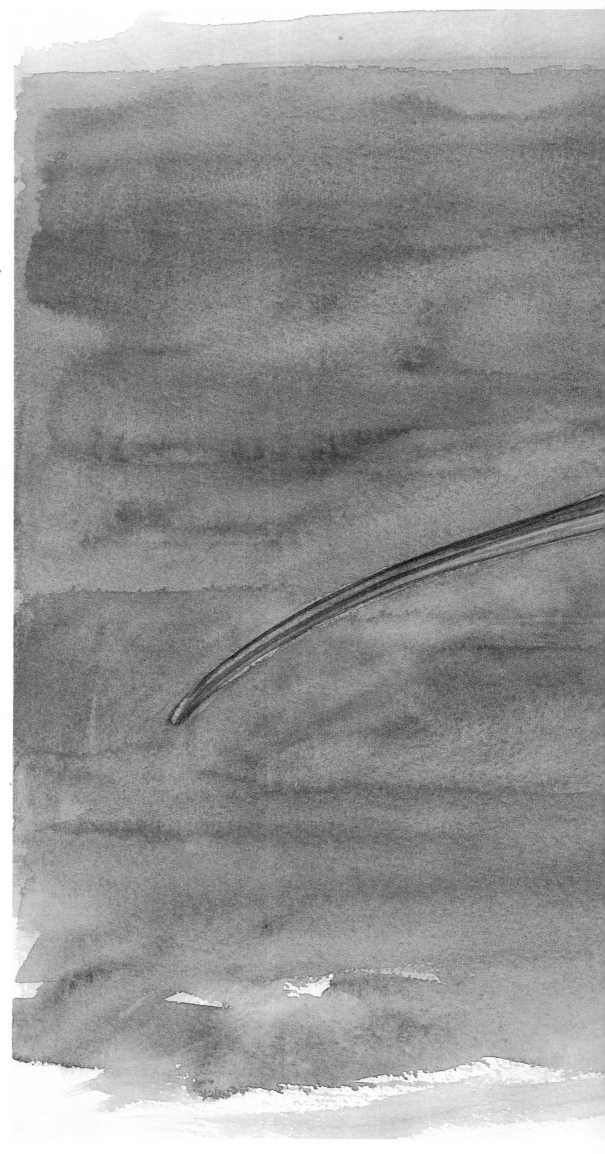

Young Curlew

2 August

A peace, a strange peace rests over the island. The wind is southerly and has the warmth of summer. The day could pass unnoticed if the contrast with previous days were not so keenly felt. The silence – all the calls and the intense activity are missing. The wind too adds its part, for it is blowing away from the island. Life on the island is now characterised by expectation and suspense. Rather mopingly the birds stand asleep facing the wind, preen now and then or seek food. The new feathers growing out claim all the Avocets', Ringed Plovers' and Black-headed Gulls' strength. The terns are considerably fewer, only a Common Tern, three Sandwich and two Little Terns during the whole day. A pair of Caspian Terns also; they rasp harshly from inside the bay and circle high on one occasion. Like migrating buzzards, they soar up under the thickening cumulus clouds.

I notice that the Common Tern has two lighter spots in front of and above the eye, the first sign that its black forehead has served its purpose and is turning to winter white. When I sweep my eyes over the island and see how most birds are resting, collapsed behind tufts of seaweed and in hollows, I realise how much their colours are losing their lustre. They lose their liveliness in the same way as does the breeding season's boisterous fervour, and with it the bright aggressive signals, contrasts in black and white and red bills. Everything is diluted and disappears in the same way as the birds. The individuals, the characters, handsome and showy defenders of territories and young, sink into the oneness of the collective body. A new phase is coming.

When at about five o'clock in the afternoon I hear a Turnstone, I am struck by their absence. The groups and small flocks that were here only one week ago are already on their way. Perhaps the island's Turnstones are even now standing on some Dutch shore at low tide or on a reef of rocks in Brittany.

An adult Sanderling still with a rust-coloured breast takes a break for a quarter of an hour. Somewhat restlessly, it searches between the northwest and the cove and picks among strips of sea foam on the level shore. Several times it stands bill facing southwest. It waits for the drop from the sky that will trigger off onward migration and then it disappears, with slightly clipping wings while uttering one or two short 'tjitt' . . . 'tjütt' calls. I look up at the sky and listen for the drop, that is a relative that may be passing, but nothing can be heard. Not all can be interpreted.

Half-grown Ringed Plover chick

Sanderling

3 August

A Robinson Crusoe came to the island today. The sea is full of shipwrecked souls seeking for firm land. Insects, flower seeds and all kinds of small animals drift about a precarious existence. Most succumb, but a few find their island, a place where life is possible. I discover it only a metre off the southeast tip, bobbing rather listlessly in the gentle eddies around the little reef, a whole clump of scentless mayweed. It has obviously been torn away from some other shore and then sailed around finally like so many other things to end up in the island's waters. After a quarter of an hour it has run aground on the shoreline and the waves push it up short distances, at the same time as it packs itself down in the sand. The clump is full of flowers, but it has the appearance that one would associate with shipwreck victims, wet through, tortured by the wind, tattered and torn and weary in the stems. It nevertheless finds a foothold and blossoms out again when the water level drops in the next few days; the island has got a new inhabitant. It attracts insects, and several times Wood Sandpipers find edible items in its recesses.

The sandy shore is an insecure place, and few are the plants that succeed in adapting to the salt and the extreme variations between drought and flooding. On the other hand, the sea is generous with food and constantly washes up parts of dead plants and animals which release nitrogen and phosphorus. Scentless mayweed usually grows most abundantly on well-fertilised arable and cattle pasture and may seem to have an impossible environment on the island. The arable land and the sand beach nevertheless have their similarities: good food supply and rigorous stirring up are common denominators – the arable land is ploughed and the waves turn over the sand.

White Wagtail on the warmest day of the year.
The grass-leaved orache sways like a palm on a South
Pacific island and affords shade to humble folk

Young Little Ringed Plover

Young Ringed Plover

Grey Plover, a female

5 August

Perhaps the warmest day of the year, not directly oppressive but simply warm. The wind is in the west and light. The ladybirds are swarming. They settle everywhere and not least on the body, where they bite at regular intervals. My dog Columbus and I take a walk and then sit down right out on the point in order to get the coolness from the sea. On the island I count thirty-one Ringed Plovers and one Little Ringed Plover. Many are squatting down and in the heat haze they almost disappear into the sand and seaweed.

While I am counting a Grey Plover flies over. I try to call it down by whistling, but it is altogether too determined.

The Little Ringed Plover really is little, and its head appears to be only half as big as the Ringed Plover's. It is dainty, more lacking in contrast in the face, and with longer wings. In the heat haze only the general outline is clear, but this accentuates the two species' differences; the Little is like a pointer among a pack of boxers.

6 August

The Redshank flocks are quite large now and gathered for the journey south. I count thirty-two individuals in one flock which, while uttering intense 'tju-hu' and 'tju-hu-hu' calls, make a sweep over the bay. Otherwise the late afternoon is very quiet. Just as the breeze subsides in the limpid hour between afternoon and evening, so the birds also appear to bide their time for the evening's activity. During this 'glass hour', the passage between afternoon and evening, the light is still strong and dazzling but the colours acquire a different intensity and one notices the increasing length of the shadows. It is now that we humans make a move from the beach, begin to think about and make plans for the evening; our stomachs make themselves felt. And it is now that the cows decide to make their way in to the pasture in the bay; in a long string they plod in to the shallow water past the island.

The evening comes, but slowly. My cheek facing the sea becomes cool; the one facing the west and the sun burns, and tells me that my face is flushed with colour. The calls of the waders increase. Most intense are the large waders, the *Tringa*, Redshank, Wood Sandpiper, isolated Greenshanks and Spotted Redshanks, for they all migrate by night.

When the sky in the west is whitish yellow-pink, the sea towards the east becomes turquoise and the sky at its zenith soft blue. The flying terns take on and reflect these tones and shades. They undulate and bodies and wings change places as in a finely tuned kaleidoscope according to wing beats and flight direction. In this way the birds capture the sky and the colours of the sea. A poetic interpretation – no, a fact, it is quite simply why they are white, that is what nature intends. What my senses experience and my intellect transcribes as inconceivable is for nature a matter of course; the miracle is a law of nature.

Wood Sandpiper at dusk

7 August

It is four o'clock; a pink band in the east, small narrow almond clouds have rapidly sparkling neon-pink underedges. The Avocets are still sleeping heavily, up to their knees in the water. But many of the birds have woken up and left the island of sleep in order to seek food. A Curlew calls for a long time, plaintively, as if it cannot decide whether it will leave the bay or not. At about half past four fifteen Barnacle Geese come in from the territory in the northeast, yelping, gliding in handsome formation.

Quarter past five. Suddenly the sun comes up. I am lying in the sand on the island, and can see it grow like a mushroom from the same perspective as the birds. In a way I am not prepared for it, it seems unreal, unreal as a set-piece from a film. The sun is reflected between the crests of the waves, shining yellow-orange. Mild but moist, the wind sweeps in. I turn on to my back and look straight up into the sky. The sky's canopy is never so round, so embracing as when one lies on the ground in an open flat landscape, and especially when one is close to the sea. The air is so mild that everything can happen, as in the moment of creation. The clouds take form, billow and meander slowly in the sea of air as if in rapture at the advent of a new day. The uppermost parts quickly acquire a faintly gleaming, cool whitish-orange colour. We know that the sun will reach us all, light up each cloud. High up there, three Swallows are flying past, perhaps at 200–300 metres altitude, and barely visible. I wonder whether the insect life up there is more abundant or whether they are simply on their way south.

At regular intervals isolated calls can be heard. Not high-level or intense calls, for the morning contained nothing of migration unrest. I note down a Curlew, a Ringed Plover, Dunlins, a Sandwich Tern, whistling wings from a group of Shelducks, Meadow Pipit. Calls and sounds accumulate in the sea, irregularly but nevertheless with a kind of natural, easy rhythm – they belong here. Ten past seven. Nine Common Terns migrate southwest, followed by an additional six and two.

Seven Curlews move southwest, and the lone bird that had been calling all morning at last receives a reply. It goes up to meet the flock and tacks on to a well-formed line that is travelling as one, sights set on its destination, towards the southwest.

Young Starling that has started to moult

Starling ejecting a pellet

9 August

The sun is a couple of inches above the horizon. The island is in contact with the land. Large platforms of sand lie spread out like delta lands in towards the shore and facing the outer side. A wooden box has been uncovered on the north beach, and on the spit towards the shore nearest to me there is something green-looking, shining somewhat like an emerald. To tell the truth, I have never seen an emerald as far as I know, but before me I see a deep, slightly transparent, obscurely bright green colour. Curaçao is perhaps better, green curaçao shines in the channel on my tropical romantic island.

Ten moulting Ruffs rest in the cove together with seven Curlew Sandpipers and a score of Dunlins.

Later in the day a crowd of Starlings come and look for food in the seaweed.

10 August

I come to a summer bay; sunny but with good visibility and fresh, a little touch of September in the air, a light easterly wind and cumulus stacked up high against the sky. It is silent and there are few birds on the island, perhaps because my neighbour is repairing a boat close by.

A flock of Common Terns, twenty-four individuals, four Black Terns and a Little Gull come in from the bay, round the point and fly confidently southwards.

Towards nightfall a Hooded Crow alights somewhat surprisingly on the island just off the banks. With rolling gait, it searches over the sand bottom which is uncovered by the low water. In between pecking in some clump of seaweed or a shell, it looks rather suspiciously in my direction and very quickly disappears. In the clear air and the slanting light it acquires a remarkable irradiance. This is the first time I have seen a Hooded Crow visit the island.

Hooded Crow

12 August

A crowd of Black-headed Gulls doze on the north tip. The Avocets are quietly dabbling about for food. Summer lull and the air is almost completely silent.

15 August

When I arrive seven Great Black-backed Gulls are standing on the large bank – marvellous! Three of them take wing immediately, but the others linger for a minute or so in tense posture before they too make off in the direction of the bay. Only when one comes really close to Great Black-backed Gulls does one realise their imposing size, like large buzzards. The last few days have been quite calm, so it is with a certain surprise that I find that there are plenty of resting birds, mostly Dunlins but also two Curlew Sandpipers, Ruffs and the first young Little Stint.

The Oystercatcher is walking with its now fully grown young one on the large bank. They walk close together and the young appears still to be somewhat dependent; it crouches in a begging posture on a couple of occasions, but without success.

A young Common Gull struggles rather hopefully through the wind on slightly bowed wings. Its grey and dirty-looking tones are softened, the only thing they can be in a dry sunny wind. When it passes over the sand of the island it takes on an intense warm lighting from below, so that each little marking and shading stands out.

There is a dead bird lying on the shoreline by the west point; I cannot see what it is. It looks at first glance to be in two parts. The most obvious thing is a wing which is being rocked rather gently in the waves; it looks relatively dark. A young Black-headed Gull or Shelduck, I guess.

Warm and sunny, a dry and fresh westerly wind – I enjoy the day.

16 August

Sun, but following morning rain. The air is like velvet – who could not be affected by it? There is nothing like the soft, clean oxygen-rich air after thundery rain. One just stands and breathes, inhales and savours each life-giving breath. The wind gets its moistness and saltiness from the sea; it picks up the tang of seaweed when it reaches land; there it is quickly warmed up and takes on with the fragrance of thyme and dry grass.

A hundred Dunlins and five Knots were standing on the island. The water round about is steel-grey and mirrors the large, slightly grey cumulus clouds that are sailing away to the northeast. Each fragment of seaweed, each shell on the island is crystal clear in outline. I let my gaze run through the telescope, see how the seaweed has crept farther and farther in over the sand, stop at a feather that is lightly quivering in the wind, and suddenly come across an unfamiliar face – a Sanderling. It is rather dirty-grey, probably a female, with piebald summer plumage and only sparse rust-coloured touches on the sides of the breast. It runs along the far side, picks in the sand, dashes farther, meets a Little Stint which it joins for a few yards. Some unrecognised silhouette in the sky gets all waders on the wing and I never see the Sanderling again. But all of a sudden two Grey Plovers are standing there and capture my attention. The idea for a sketch of the Sanderling is promptly erased by the Grey Plovers, full of character equalled by few others.

Fledged Ringed Plover chick

Female Grey Plover

17 August

Today autumn is in the air. Clear, bright air reminding me of quiet September days. The wind is fresh and all birds sheltering behind the ridge, facing in to the wind: two Sandwich Terns, ten Little Terns, several Arctic Terns and young Black-headed Gulls. It seems too quiet for me to come down to the island. The Redshank's alarm calls are less shrill; their young are starting to stand on their own feet. Oddly, in spite of the autumnal nip, a sunny day – but that is how it is.

Things happen unnoticed and in an uncanny way. The shore goose-foots have burst into flower out on the island. Grey-green leaf cymes which have grown visible in only a few days. They spill out over the sand. From my worm's eye-view I see parts of isolated runners or ground shoots with small leaf rosettes out on the sandy heath. They tell that there is a living pattern, a network of feelers creeping over the island, sucking downwards into the sand and binding the island, stabilising it. Here an infrastructure is established which makes it possible for a new community to be built. On one part of the shore a solitary young Wheatear makes a few hops after insects. From out at sea a butterfly, a small white, comes in and passes close above the sand. Its wavering flight is emphasised by the shadow that bounces over the hollows and ridges of the sand. A young Sandwich Tern gives it a bemused glance.

There is a feather lying in the sand; it attracts my attention. Fresh, soft, as if it departed this life in its prime, like a young Sleeping Beauty. The shore is full of feathers which have been discarded to be replaced by new ones. The discarded ones are worn out, faded and bleached. They sink in among shells and stones like a part of nature's refuse, but not so this one. It is a tail feather of a young Herring Gull and its even outer web and soft, slightly yellowish-grey quill shaft tell that its wearer was born only a few months earlier and has now probably died. It should not have been moulted until next year.

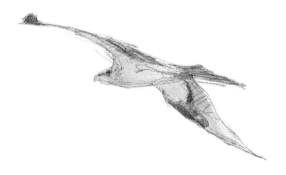

19 August

At migration times there is always a certain excitement in the air, time for the unexpected. Usually gulls and terns reveal in good time the arrival of a bird of prey, but the island was comparatively deserted today; perhaps that was the explanation of why I was taken by surprise.

A large shadow suddenly sweeps in from behind over the shore meadow. The bird is so big and so close that, although I see it only out of the corner of my eye, I immediately perceive something enormous against the sky; I look up – an Osprey. Carefully on the look-out with its wings in the wind, but a little clumsily, it glides out towards the island, turns and alights on a boulder. I get it in my telescope, really close, dishevelled, wild and with orange-yellow eyes. For several seconds the bird penetrates the whole of my being, before it takes wing as a result of my being so near. I am lucky: it takes a few wing strokes, glides and lands again a bit farther away on a rock. There it sits, eyeing its surroundings with curiosity; it was born this year. The large feet with spongy pads and grotesque long deeply curved claws are adapted for holding slippery fish and, when it comes to perching, are best suited to gripping tree branches. It has to take a few steps before it puts its equipment in order and balances its body.

When it takes off again, it allows the wind to carry it in circles high up in the sky. A Common Gull makes a few light-hearted attacks on it. The Osprey is, however, no threat to birds and seldom attracts anything other than apathetic mobbing of a somewhat routine nature. In gliding flight it turns off towards the southwest and disappears from my field of view – it is on migration.

Young Osprey, an unexpected visit

20 August

The air is saturated; it is relatively warm and calm after several days of strong wind.

A light grey sky shades in the east into a blue-grey bank of cloud, a darker solid effect with a light blue tone, almost turquoise. There is a dense wall of tensions whose extent I can only imagine and whose outline I am unable to distinguish. Above this bank a row of small lighter grey-blue clouds is brewing up, like an advance guard. At the same time the sun comes out, softly fading in so that the contrasts increase and the shadows darken. Up above in the sky and to the west, there are large clouds coming. Rather vaguely outlined above, but all with an even lead-grey base which forms an extended serpentine shape a few inches above the horizon. They expand imperceptibly, bulge out their stomachs, roll in slow motion, menacing but near and obvious so that I can perceive their character clearly. At this moment the sky is blue between these cloud masses. Here and there almost unashamed blue, but bridges of high thin cloud join the stormy weather in the east with that in the west. These light cirrus clouds, vibrant in their frailty, do not feel secure. I imagine how quickly they can be added to, darken and be impregnated with the surrounding tensions. Right here where the sun is forcing its way through with its friendly warmth, the bad weather will advance. Here the accumulated weight of the cloud masses will come falling down when the apparently inevitable downpour takes place. Powers which are natural, but nevertheless seem divorced from the natural order of things, can change the scene overnight.

The sea bites into the shoreline. I feel that at any time the island, my reality, can turn out to be a sunken rock, a ripple on the surface, an insignificant token of what once existed, an obituary on something to whose beauty only this witness can testify. I am frightened and wonder at it all.

22 August

Deserted, windy, with thick grey clouds across the sky. The thought that only a couple of weeks earlier I was sitting in shorts and now and then running off for a bathe feels foreign, it seems to be several months ago. The island is reduced to a sand shoal. A few Ringed Plovers, two Common Sandpipers and a single Redshank are resting; they are no longer at home. Perhaps there will be new summer days to come? There is a strange feeling of universality about the autumn. The birds are in the act of departing and have been partially shaken out of their routines. The place no longer affords them a home environment or secluded space. The air is clear and fresh, the birds pass, are on their way, like passers by in a big city.

I look out over the sea just when the sun bursts down between the large grey clouds. A ship passes a long way off but with only the upper part visible above the horizon, careening in the waves, like a mirage with evasive and flickering contours. The whole time birds are moving past and all going in the same direction – southwards.

Three Common Terns fly past; I follow them in my telescope until they disappear far away in the distance, perhaps the last ones I shall see this year.

Young Black-headed Gull

27/8-81

An idea formed in my mind. In October–
November when autumn storms are
raging, I would go down and see the island
disappear, see Atlantis sink in the ocean. But
come the thirty-first of August . . . The
island has gone. It has been blowing hard
from the southeast, and everything is gone.
Only an impersonal strip of sand that gleams
in the choppy sea.

A young Ringed Plover tries to land but is
constantly forced on to the wing by the
washing waves. It has a searching look on its
face. Can it possibly be one of the Ringed
Plover young that grew up here and is now
looking for something that it knows was
here?

But when it returns next spring it will find a
new sand shoal, a new formation . . . But *the
island*, that is gone for ever.

Young Ringed Plover

Photo: Ragnhild Erlandsson

Lars Jonsson was born in 1952 and grew up in Stockholm. Nowadays he is for the most part resident in southern Gotland. During the whole of his childhood he drew and painted; at fifteen years of age he made his debut with an exhibition at the National Museum of Natural History that attracted much attention. He is self-taught.

As a bird artist Lars Jonsson is world-renowned. During the 1970s he illustrated and wrote five field handbooks on the birds of Europe. These books have aroused great interest all around the world, and have been published in seven different countries outside Sweden.

Lars Jonsson has shown his art in exhibitions at galleries and museums in Sweden, England and the USA. In 1982 his picture of the Gyrfalcon on the 50-kronor postage stamp was selected as the most beautiful stamp of the year.

He has been portrayed in and has contributed to Swedish and international daily press, specialist literature, radio and TV. Now more engagements are awaiting him in the USA with exhibitions, graphic publications and assignments as guest lecturer at seminars in bird painting.

Of his book Bird Island, he himself says: The water colours and the discourses in Bird Island emanate from an intoxicated inspiration, they are impressions from the island's short life during an intense summer.